I Wanted to Know All about God

by Virginia L. Kroll

illustrated by Debra Reid Jenkins

William B. Eerdmans Publishing Company
Grand Rapids, Michigan

Library of Congress Cataloging-in-Publication Data

Kroll, Virginia L.
I wanted to know all about God / by Virginia L. Kroll ;
illustrated by Debra Reid Jenkins.
p.   cm.
ISBN 0-8028-5078-2
1. God—Juvenile literature. [1. God.] I. Jenkins,
Debra Reid, ill. II. Title.
BT107.K767 1994

231—dc20   93-37382
                                                              CIP
                                                               AC

For my husband
David Haeick,
with love.
        —V.K.

For Garth and Puzzle,
with love.
        —debra

I wanted to know all about God,
so I went out looking for Him in signs of His creation.

I wondered what God does in the mornings.
Then I smelled the dew on the grass at dawn.

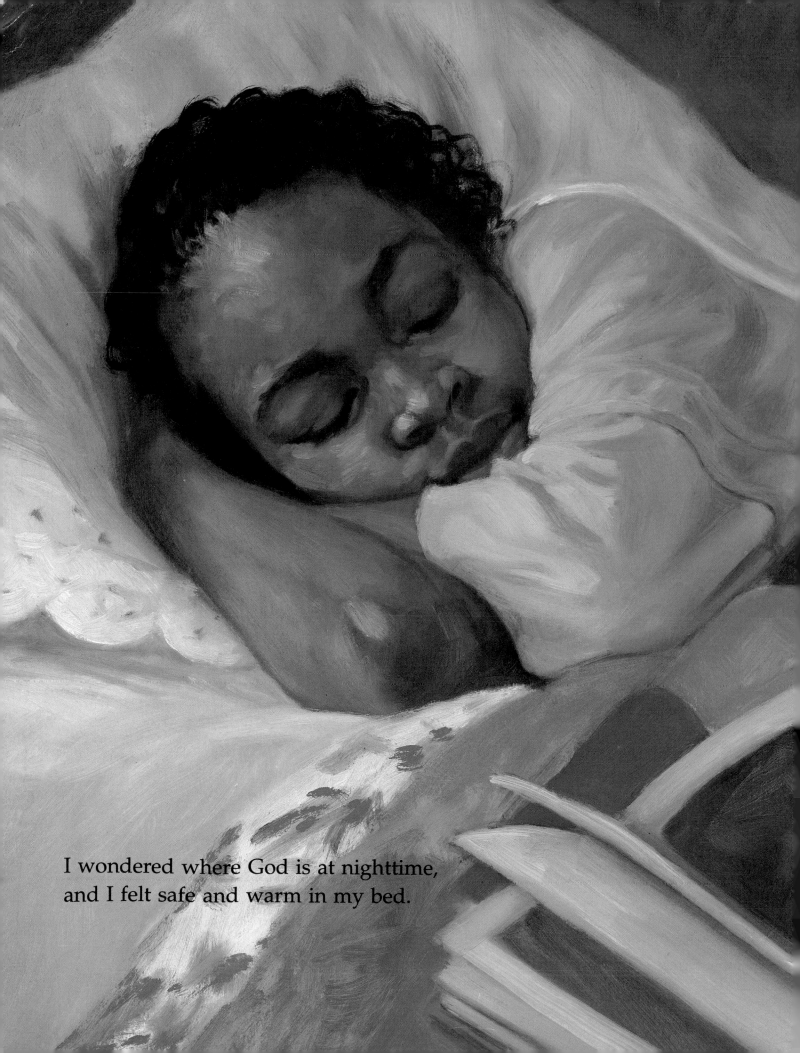

I wondered where God is at nighttime,
and I felt safe and warm in my bed.

I wondered if God is gentle,
and a butterfly floated on the air in front of me.

I wondered if God is strong,
and the ocean roared in my ears.

I wondered how God's reflection
looks when he smiles,
and the snow glittered in the sun.

I wanted to know if God likes music.
Then I heard a pond on a summer night.

I wondered if God likes art,
and I saw a spiderweb in my uncle's barn.

I wanted to know what colors God likes.
Then I met several children of other races.

I wondered how tall God makes his people,
and the girl next to me looked up and smiled.

I wondered if God's people have faith in each other,
and my friend trusted me with a secret.

I wondered if God is caring,
and the new boy shared his crayons with me.

I wondered what God's love feels like,
and Grandma put her arms around me
and gave me a big hug.

I wanted to know where God likes to visit,
and I felt someone knocking at my heart.
Now when I go out looking for God,
I know exactly where to find Him.